EDGE
BOOKS™

SURVIVAL
FACTS OR FIBS

KRISTIN J. RUSSO

CAPSTONE PRESS
a capstone imprint

Edge Books are published by Capstone Press,
1710 Roe Crest Drive
North Mankato, Minnesota 56003
www.mycapstone.com

Library of Congress Cataloging-in-Publication Data
Library of Congress Cataloging-in-Publication data is available on the Library of Congress website.
ISBN 978-1-5435-0206-0 (library binding)
ISBN 978-1-5435-0210-7 (paperback)
ISBN 978-1-5435-0214-5 (eBook PDF)

Editorial Credits
Editor: Lauren Dupuis-Perez
Book Designer: Sara Radka
Production Specialist: Kathy McColley

Image Credits
Getty Images, Buena Vista Images, background, cover (background), Chessie Racing/ALLSPORT, 17, David McNew, 25, Flickr RF, 18, Floortje, 16, Frederick Bass, 29, Joseph Van Os, 26, Glowimages, 22, hadynyah, 10, Hemera, 15, Lezh, 24, Michael Blann, 23, Moment RF, 8, 12, 21, Pavliha, 13, PeopleImages, cover , stock_colors, 4; iStockphoto: Chalabala, 6, Elenathewise, 7, Erik_Eiser, 14, gutaper, 27 (bottom), iammotos, 11, back cover, JoKMedia, 27 (top), SvetaP, 9, ValerijaP, 28, vchal, 20; Newscom: Dale O'Dell Stock Connection Worldwide, 19

Graphic elements by Capstone Press and Book Buddy Media.

The publisher does not endorse products whose logos may appear on objects in images in this book.

Printed and bound in the USA.
010878S18

TABLE OF CONTENTS

SURVIVAL

A desert's extreme daytime and nighttime temperatures can be very dangerous.

Early humans thought of ways to survive the dangers of the world. The human imagination helps people survive when food, water, and shelter are hard to find.

Even today people can sometimes find themselves in danger. They may be lost in the woods. Sometimes they are in a risky situation, such as an earthquake, tornado, or fire. Rescue agencies will try to help people in these situations. But sometimes people must rely on their own survival skills.

Some people seek out danger on purpose. They are thrill-seekers and adventurers. They test their skills in difficult survival situations. These thrill-seekers climb mountains. They explore underground caves. They camp in dangerous **habitats**. Sometimes they swim or scuba dive in ocean areas that they know will be treacherous.

Humans are champions at adapting to new situations. We face dangers similar to those survived by early humans. We also face man-made dangers. Through culture and technology we find new ways to survive and thrive.

• • • • • • • • • • • • • • • • • • • •

habitat—the natural place and conditions in which a plant or animal lives

CHAPTER 1
SURVIVING IN THE WOODS

Creating a signal to stand out in the woods can help direct rescuers to your location. Rescuers will know they're getting close if they see something out of the ordinary.

IT'S TRUE! White pine needles are a natural source of Vitamin C. Making a tea with white pine needles will boost your immune system and help avoid malnutrition.

Many people enjoy camping and exploring the woods. If a person gets lost, it's important to know what to do first.

FACT OR FIB?

People who are lost in the woods should search for a food source first.

Evidence

It is tempting for hungry wanderers to search for food first. This may not be necessary if a prepared camper has brought along snacks. However, some people who get lost are not prepared. In this case, survival experts say that food will become an important priority. But should it be first?

Answer: FIB

People can live for weeks, or even months, without food. They can only live for up to a week without water. Survival experts suggest looking for lifesaving resources in this order: shelter, water, fire, and then food. Without shelter and warmth, a victim might die within 24 hours of **hypothermia**.

What if you are lost in the woods with no shelter? Use material that is easily found in the forest, such as wood. People can find shelter in hollow trees. They can also build rough shelters with tree **saplings**. They can use leaves to help keep rainwater out.

. . . .

hypothermia—a life-threatening condition that occurs when a person's body temperature falls several degrees below normal

sapling—a young tree

Drinking water from a still pond without the proper tools is never a good idea.

In the wilderness, even clean-looking water could be dangerous. It is impossible to tell if drinking water is safe just by looking at it. Campers and hikers who have planned ahead bring water with them. They may also bring **purification** tablets. These tablets kill harmful bacteria. They make water safe to drink in about 30 minutes. They are available at sporting goods stores and pharmacies.

IT'S TRUE!

Hypothermia is a very dangerous condition. People lose body heat quickly from the head and neck. Adventurers in cold climates should cover their heads to prevent heat loss.

FACT OR FIB?

You must boil water for at least 10 minutes to make it safe to drink.

Evidence

Unprepared people who are lost in the woods must drink water from ponds, lakes, or streams. This water may contain bacteria or parasites that can make a person sick. To make it safe to drink, many people boil water for 10 minutes.

Answer: FIB

It does not take 10 minutes to kill off dangerous bacteria and parasites. Boiling water for up to three minutes is enough to make it safe.

If you're going to boil water, you'll need a fire. To build a fire without matches, gather dry twigs and **tinder**. Using the smaller twigs, create a standing triangle with tinder placed in the center. Use a lens from a pair of eyeglasses, binoculars, or a camera. Concentrate the sun's rays on the tinder until it smokes and sparks.

Dig a small hole and line it with dirt and clay. Fill the hole with water. Heat rocks with the fire. When the rocks are hot enough, move them with a strong stick into the small pool of water. The hot rocks will boil the water.

purification—the process of making something clean
tinder—dry material, such as wood or grass, that burns easily

9

CHAPTER 2
SURVIVING IN THE DESERT

Keep your mouth closed or covered if you must walk in the desert. This slows breathing and can help prevent **dehydration**.

People should never go into a desert without enough water to survive. In the desert the human body needs about 1 gallon (3.8 liters) of water a day. Some people who are lost in a desert think about drinking their own **urine**.

IT'S TRUE! In the Atacama Desert in Chile, about 0.5 inch (1.3 centimeters) of rain falls each year. People there harvest fog in special mesh screens. The screens catch droplets of moisture. They collect enough water this way to take showers and grow flowers.

FACT OR FIB?

Drinking your own urine will help you stay hydrated.

Evidence

Even thrill-seekers who are prepared to explore desert **environments** can get into trouble. If they run out of water some people may drink urine.

Answer: UNDECIDED

If a person has recently had water, their urine is about 95 percent water. In that case urine will help them survive. But people who suffer from **dehydration** do not have urine with a high water content. Their urine contains higher levels of waste materials such as nitrogen, potassium, and calcium. These materials will stress their kidneys.

People can live about a week without water. If they can drink urine people can add a few days to their survival.

urine—a body's liquid waste
hydrate—to achieve a healthy balance of fluids in the body
environment—the natural world of the land, water, and air
dehydration—a condition that occurs when someone loses more fluids than he or she takes in

Extreme heat and lack of water are huge risks to people in the desert. Another extreme danger that few people are aware of is stormy weather.

FACT OR FIB?

A sandstorm is one of the biggest dangers in a desert.

Evidence

The Sahara is a desert in Africa. It is the largest hot desert on Earth, and it is very dry. The Sahara may get rain twice in one week, and then not again for the next three years! It gets fewer than 3 inches (7.6 cm) of rain per year. This means that the desert sand is almost always loose and dry.

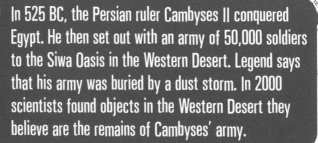

IT'S TRUE! In 525 BC, the Persian ruler Cambyses II conquered Egypt. He then set out with an army of 50,000 soldiers to the Siwa Oasis in the Western Desert. Legend says that his army was buried by a dust storm. In 2000 scientists found objects in the Western Desert they believe are the remains of Cambyses' army.

If you see a sandstorm on the horizon, you may be able to avoid it. Your best chance to avoid a sandstorm is to run or drive away from it as fast as you can.

Answer: FACT

When strong winds blow over loose soil or sand, they can cause a sandstorm. Sandstorms are also called dust storms. In the Sahara, sand dunes rise as high as 500 to 600 feet (150 to 180 meters). The dunes are constantly blown around by the high winds.

Scorching winds can sometimes whip up huge sandstorms without warning, blinding travelers. During a sandstorm, people can barely breathe. To protect themselves, people will wrap a scarf or bandana around their heads and faces. Sandstorms can be over quickly or last for days.

CHAPTER 3

SURVIVING IN THE OCEAN

Rip currents reach speeds up to 8 feet (2.4 m) per second. That's almost twice as fast as an Olympic swimmer.

Rip currents are responsible for more than 100 deaths in the United States each year. Eighty percent of beach rescues are related to rip currents. These currents are also known as riptides. They are powerful, narrow currents that pull swimmers from the surf zone farther into the ocean.

IT'S TRUE! Two Japanese men hold the record for surviving the longest amount of time at sea. They were at sea for 484 days. Their ship was damaged in a storm. The men were rescued in March of 1815. They survived by eating their ship's cargo, soybeans, and drinking distilled seawater. Twelve other crew members died.

Swimmers caught in a riptide should always swim **parallel** to the shore.

WARNING

HIGH SURF

Can cause serious injuries or drowning
IF IN DOUBT, DON'T GO OUT

WARNING

RIP CURRENTS
You could be swept out
and drown
IF IN DOUBT, DON'T GO OUT

Evidence

Many people believe that swimming with the current is best. They think that it will eventually bring them back to shore. But in fact, a riptide could cause the swimmer to drift farther and farther away from the shore.

Answer: FACT

Some swimmers can escape if they swim out of a riptide. They swim parallel to the shore. If someone is swimming directly against the current, they will lose energy and will eventually drift out to sea. Swim along the shoreline and eventually you will swim out of the rip current.

parallel—having the same direction or course as another object

April 15, 1912, is the date of a famous **maritime** disaster. The luxury ocean liner *Titanic* sank after hitting an iceberg. There were about 2,200 people on board. Only 705 survived on lifeboats.

The story of the *Titanic* is famous. But shipwrecks and maritime disasters are not unusual. Boaters often face dangers and must make decisions about survival. The survivors of the *Titanic* waited a few hours for rescue. What if stranded passengers and crew have to wait for days?

FACT OR FIB?

It is okay to drink salt water if you are adrift at sea.

Evidence

Ocean water contains salt. The amount of salt is measured in parts per million (ppm). Freshwater has fewer than 1,000 ppm of salt. Ocean water contains about 35,000 ppm of salt.

IT'S TRUE! About 70 percent of Earth's surface is covered with water. Scientists know more about the moon's surface than the deepest parts of the ocean. In fact, 12 people have stepped foot on the moon, but only 3 have been to the Mariana Trench. This undersea valley's deepest point is about 7 miles (11 kilometers) deep.

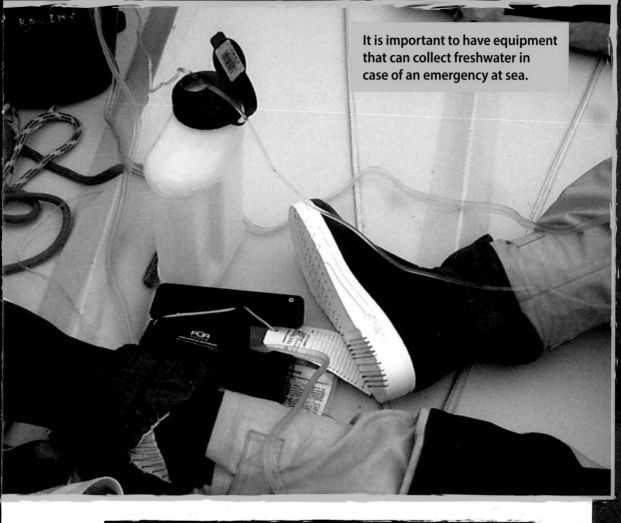

It is important to have equipment that can collect freshwater in case of an emergency at sea.

Answer: FIB

When people drink salt water, their kidneys work harder to filter out the extra salt. This causes people to die from dehydration.

Salt water can be turned into drinkable water. The process is called **desalination**. Special desalination equipment should always be available on board a boat or ship.

. . . .

maritime—related to the sea, ships, or sea travel

desalination—the process of removing the salt from ocean water

CHAPTER 4
SURVIVING IN EXTREME WEATHER

Lightning flashes about 40 times per second worldwide.

A lightning bolt can travel between clouds, from a cloud into the air, or from a cloud to the ground. It opens up a small channel in the air. After the electricity passes, the air collapses back into the open space. This makes the crackling sound of thunder.

Lightning can strike as far as 10 miles (16 km) from the center of a storm. It may not even be raining yet when lighting strikes. It is important to head indoors during a thunder and lightning storm. If you are outside, avoid wide-open fields or standing near the tallest object. Lightning is attracted to tall trees or lampposts. Waiting out a storm inside a car is also a safe option.

FACT OR FIB?

Most lightning strikes are fatal.

Evidence

When a person is struck by lightning, electrical energy moves across and through their bodies. The powerful electricity causes burns and other injuries. These injuries can be very serious.

Answer: FIB

Only 10 percent of lightning strikes are fatal. That means 90 percent of people struck by lightning survive. Some people recover quickly. Others have permanent injuries. A victim of a lightning strike should seek medical attention immediately.

IT'S TRUE!

U.S. park ranger Roy Sullivan was hit by lightning seven times between 1942 and 1977. He survived each strike.

A tornado is a **rotating** column of air. They are more common in some areas than in others. Tornadoes can have wind speeds up to 300 miles (480 km) per hour. They can stretch more than 2 miles (3.2 km) wide. Extreme tornadoes stay on or near the ground for up to 100 miles (160 km).

FACT OR FIB?

Tornadoes only take place in "Tornado Alley" in the United States.

Evidence

Tornadoes can destroy large buildings. They can uproot trees. They can hurl vehicles and other large items into the air. In Tornado Alley it is easy for cold air and warm air to mix. This creates ideal conditions for tornadoes.

IT'S TRUE!

Tornadoes can pick up cars and vans that weigh around 3,000 pounds (1,360 kilograms). Other heavier objects, like freight-train cars, can be knocked over on their sides.

rotate—to spin around

Kansas has at least one tornado most months. The worst tornado for Kansas was in 1955. It caused 80 deaths and 270 injuries.

Answer: FIB

Tornadoes occur everywhere on Earth except Antarctica. It is true that many tornadoes take place in Tornado Alley. Tornado Alley includes sections of Texas, Oklahoma, Kansas, and Nebraska in the United States.

Canada has the second most reported tornadoes on Earth. Five percent of the world's tornadoes take place on the prairies of Canada each year.

CHAPTER 5

SURVIVING FIRE

Kitchen grease fires, heating, and electrical malfunctions are the most common causes of accidental house fires.

House fires can spread quickly. Say a fire ignites by an unattended candle. About one minute after a fire starts, it has grown rapidly and smoke fills the room. It is tempting to flee a burning building by running out the front door. But is it the safest way to escape?

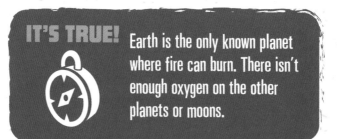

IT'S TRUE! Earth is the only known planet where fire can burn. There isn't enough oxygen on the other planets or moons.

Running out the door is the best way to escape a house fire.

Evidence

Only two and a half minutes after the fire starts, smoke spreads through the house. One minute later, a **flashover** can take place. The energy and heat in the original room ignites everything in it. The temperature in that room could now be close to 1,400 degrees Fahrenheit (760 degrees Celsius). Less than five minutes after the fire started, rescue may not be possible.

Answer: FIB

Smoke rises in a fire, so it is best to stay close to the floor. Covering your face and crawling quickly to an escape route is best. Also, opening a door without first checking its temperature could be dangerous. Feel a door before you open it. If it's hot, there is likely fire on the other side. Find another escape route through a window or a different door.

Firefighters advise having an escape plan ahead of time. Instincts such as running straight for the front door or hiding from the fire could be deadly.

· ·

flashover—an instance of a fire spreading very rapidly across a gap because of intense heat

Wildfires are also called bushfires or forest fires. They move quickly. With strong winds and dry ground, wildfires generally spread between 9 and 12.5 miles (14.5 and 20 km) per hour. Usually places near a wildfire are **evacuated** in time for people to get out safely. But this isn't always the case.

 **FACT OR FIB?** To escape a wildfire, dig a trench that the fire cannot cross.

Evidence

If people are caught by a wildfire there are ways to survive. One mother and her children found shelter in an animal's burrow. Other people found a large drainage pipe for refuge. They rolled in water for protection. Another man survived by jumping into his swimming pool. Fire spread around him and destroyed his neighbor's home. These people were lucky.

 **IT'S TRUE!** According to the U.S. Forest Service, unattended campfires are one of the most common causes of wildfires. Other causes include fireworks, sparks from equipment or vehicles, burning leaves or debris, and cigarettes.

evacuate—to leave a dangerous place and go somewhere safer

Answer: FIB

Wildfires can jump trenches, streams, and even rivers. Hiding in a trench will not necessarily provide safety. There are ways to escape a wildfire. Evacuating immediately upwind, or against the wind, will give the best chance at survival. It is always advised to evacuate ahead of the fire, rather than try to hide.

About 10 percent of wildfires are caused by lightning strikes. Humans cause 90 percent of wildfires.

CHAPTER 6

SURVIVING AN ANIMAL ATTACK

Even though bears are very large, the majority of their diet is made up of berries, leaves, and nuts.

Humans often build homes near areas where wildlife live. Because of this, there can be accidental contact between people and wild animals. Foxes, raccoons, deer, moose, crocodiles, and opossums are often encountered. Visits from bears are also on the rise.

According to the U.S. Park Service, the chance of being injured by a bear is approximately one in 2.1 million. You're actually more likely to be killed by a bee than a bear. But if you ever run into a bear in the wild a few tips may help you survive.

 **FACT OR FIB?**

If attacked by a wild bear, a person should run.

Evidence

Most people's first instinct is to run from danger. However, experts have different advice when it comes to bears.

Answer: FIB

Running may trigger a bear's attack response. Instead of running, experts suggest you move slowly away from the animal.

Banging pots and pans may also make the animal go away. Waving your arms above your head is a good idea too. It may make you appear larger and more of a threat to the bear. It is also smart to move upwind so the bear can identify your scent as human. Humans are not a bear's normal **prey**.

. . . .

prey—an animal that is hunted by another animal for food

In 2016 a 17-year-old gorilla had to be **euthanized** at the Cincinnati Zoo in Ohio. A toddler had fallen into its enclosure. To protect the child, zoo workers put the gorilla down.

FACT OR FIB?

Many animal attacks at zoos could be avoided if humans followed zoo rules.

Evidence

In 1994 a woman climbed two fences to get into a polar bear enclosure at the Alaska Zoo. The woman was seriously injured, but she survived. Binky the polar bear did not have to be killed in order to rescue her.

IT'S TRUE! A venomous snake does not release venom every time it bites. It can control when it releases venom. Snakes only release venom about 50 percent of the time.

euthanize—to put an animal to death by injecting it with a substance that stops its breathing or heartbeat

READ MORE

Colson, Rob. *Ultimate Survival Guide for Kids.* Richmond Hill, ON, Canada: Firefly Books, 2015.

Miles, Justin. *Ultimate Explorer Guide for Kids.* Richmond Hill, ON, Canada: Firefly Books, 2015.

Yomtov, Nel. *Adrift and Alone: True Stories of Survival at Sea.* North Mankato, Minn.: Stone Arch Books, 2016.

INTERNET SITES

Use FactHound to find Internet sites related to this book.

Visit *www.facthound.com*

Just type in 9781543502060 and go.

 Check out projects, games and lots more at
www.capstonekids.com

INDEX

Many zoos play an important role in keeping endangered species alive. Visitors to zoos should follow all rules for the animals' safety.

Please Do Not Feed the Animals

Answer: FACT

Most visitor attacks at zoos are due to the visitors not following the rules. Between 2006 and 2009, humans climbed the fence to Gu Gu the panda bear's enclosure three times at the Beijing Zoo in China. All three people were injured.

Most zoos post safety rules. Some are common sense. Some explain information that visitors may not know about the animals. To be safe at a zoo, the following tips can come in handy. Don't tease animals. Stay behind safety fences. And practice respect. These tips are especially helpful at petting zoos, where people can touch the animals.

You never know when you may find yourself in a life-threatening situation. It helps to be prepared. Knowing what is fact and what is fib may just save your life.

GLOSSARY

dehydration (dee-hy-DRAY-shuhn)—a condition that occurs when someone loses more fluids than he or she takes in

desalination (dee-sah-luh-NAY-shuhn)—the process of removing the salt from ocean water

environment (in-VY-ruhn-muhnt)—the natural world of the land, water, and air

euthanize (YOO-thuh-nyz)—to put an animal to death by injecting it with a substance that stops its breathing or heartbeat

evacuate (i-VA-kyuh-wayt)—to leave a dangerous place and go somewhere safer

flashover (FLASH-oh-vuhr)—an instance of a fire spreading very rapidly across a gap because of intense heat

habitat (HAB-uh-tat)—the natural place and conditions in which a plant or animal lives

hydrate (HYE-drayt)—to achieve a healthy balance of fluids in the body

hypothermia (hi-puh-THUR-mee-uh)—a life-threatening condition that occurs when a person's body temperature falls several degrees below normal

maritime (MAYR-uh-time)—related to the sea, ships, or sea travel

parallel (PA-ruh-lel)—having the same direction or course as another object

prey (PRAY)—an animal that is hunted by another animal for food

purification (pyoor-uh-fuh-KAY-shuhn)—the process of making something clean

rotate (ROH-tate)—to spin around

sapling (SAP-ling)—a young tree

tinder (TIN-duhr)—dry material, such as wood or grass, that burns easily

urine (YUR-uhn)—a body's liquid waste